CAIRN

CAIRN

Poems by
Daverick Leggett

Cairn

Published in the UK by Meridian Press 2021

ISBN 978-0-9524640-5-1

Contents

THE LIFE
WE REFUSE

The Necessary Descent

Invisible from the road
the land folds into a valley
of tumbled granite.
We step down
through twisting chambers of oak
erupting from moss-swathed boulders
through deepening vocabularies of green
toward the sound of the river.

The signals from the world we are leaving
flit above the canopy.
This is the necessary descent.
Unless we go down
through the moist creases of earth
to touch the river
and know again the source of our aliveness,
unless we go down again and again
to drink at the cold water
this unquenched thirst
will burn in our throats
at the dry moment of our death.

Here and Now

The life we refuse
will breach our defences anyway
even at the moment of death.
Don't wait that long.

In every moment there is a door
with a sign saying "Now"
waiting to be opened.
Don't hesitate, don't even knock.

Even when we turn away
we will arrive again
at the same place.
Every step we take
is toward this door.
The life we refuse
is singing to us
from the other side.

Step through.
The old life
with its comforting certainties
is not a home for the soul.
Break the furniture, run at the door
and leap into the place they call "Here".

The Wild Will Come to Claim Us

The wild will come to claim us
if not now then when we arrive
exhausted and empty, all excuses spent.

On the underground, entombed with those
who sleepwalk into death, I hear his rage.
The rattle is not the couplings of the train
but the wild man's teeth biting at his cage.

On the streets, in the bars, in living rooms
they try to kill him. I cannot sleep.
The city is intent on murder.

When he stands bleeding and howling at the door
saying "remember me?" this is what you must do.
Go with him.
Take nothing with you.
Don't look back.

Arriving at Grief

Arriving at grief
after a parched life
tears pressing up
from a slow spring
seep from eyes
dry from looking.

All these years
something there was
which never slept
urging the water
toward dormant seeds
and now at last
the patient desert
rejoices with flowers.

And the dry land says
I was always waiting
for this, only wanting this:
tears for flowers,
grief to birth the new world.

Until Now

All morning I have sat
with my back to the rock
face upstream, sun bouncing
off the reeling cascade
of the tireless water.
Above oak, rowan and ash
grapple exuberantly skyward
a buzzard circling overhead
as if held for a moment
by the line of my gaze
the wind in my face
a dipper criss cross and bobbing
above its own reflection
in the peat stained river.

When the fish leaps
making a small rainbow
I quiver with sudden knowing.
Here I could let it happen
all that I have resisted til now
the life that wants to enter me.

Raft

It comes again, the great grief
as I sit by the river
feeling the vast
acceleration of our time
toward so many
precious extinctions.

I throw stones, runes
cast against a future
I dread.

I could fall easily into its flow
let the water push me down
roll me over boulders
drown me if it will

But I am tumbled instead
bruised and gasping
to the shallows.
Today this grief
asks me to live.

The small boats I shape
from dead leaves
I give to the current.
One perhaps will serve
as priest to someone's drowning,
another be the raft
that carries them to shore.

On the riverbank
the wild garlic glistens
and celandine lie scattered
like yellow stars.
If grief is the price
of loving this world
I submit.

Pan

You can tell them by their walk, the city kids
still wearing their street smarts in the fields
their tight reflexes finding no mark
their strutting out of time
nothing to ward off here except the silence
so loud it unsettles them.

If I walked among them now stinking of forest
all hair and horn, they would not see me
so I melt into the earth, the trees, the dark riverbed
and wait.

Still they look but do not see.
The old knowing smoulders deep in their bodies
so I blow to kindle it awake.
One morning perhaps they will wake to find
what they did not know they had lost.
Until then I beat out the first rhythms
and breathe into their dreams.

Three Meetings with God

This morning
god beamed at me
from the trumpeting flower
of a daffodil
and I smiled back.

Later, walking the cliff path,
I found him hovering,
a keen falcon poised
impossibly on air.
I smiled back.

This evening
when he looked into my eyes
from the mirror
I smiled back.

Meditation

In the stillness I expected to find silence;
instead the roar of everything moving.
Nothing is still. Even the rocks
are in constant motion too slow to see.
The earth hurtles through space
great stars explode
and my little ship rides on
into an unimaginable emptiness
right here where I sit.

Aleppo

I turn from this morning's news toward a sunrise
displaying itself in a thousand breaking colours.
While I slept the sun rose in Aleppo
on dust rising from the ruins
of living rooms, of bakeries, of nurseries
shone pointlessly on severed limbs
on the flyblown wounds of children
and the gashes where mouths should have been
shone through the keening cries of mothers
and the silence of those
who can no longer
speak their grief.

And I, who am alive,
tell myself this.
The sunrise is news too
so is birdsong and the green hues of grass.
To ignore either
is to turn away from being human.
The sunrise or today's news
both can break the heart open
news too painful to bear
a sunrise too beautiful to bear.

SINGING
THE LAST SONG

Cairn

We tried at first to understand by numbers
thinking how simple it would be
but the numbers span us round
giddy, unable to hold our centre
as if they held a compact force
that repelled any approach.

And so we turned to names
and spoke them at the speed of their leaving
Spix's Macaw, Eastern Cougar, Baiji Dolphin
Pyrenean Ibex, Western Black Rhino, Zanzibar Leopard
Eskimo Curlew, Cry Violet
and on and on
until our grief choked us.

In the end we turned to piling stones
a speechless meditation on extinction
a long line of us day after day
the cairn growing impossibly
towering now
above our fragile homes.

If you listen you will hear it
the clack of stone upon stone
soundtrack to our days and nights
full stops at the end
of million year lines.

Fishing in Mauritania

The telling can be hard.
Some days imagination will not
soar in glorious unbridled flight
but must toil and sweat
in the field of its labour.

Once, a young man drenched
and blistered, my reach extended
by a new scythe, I looked down
exultant on four acres cut in swathes.
I remember this.

I remember too the combine harvesters
the line of them howling across the horizon
through clouds of dust
and how I was afraid.

Now, setting down the newspaper
I look from the small boat of my imagination
at the factory ships off Mauritania.
They say each ship takes into its jaws
more fish in one day
than a local boat will catch in a lifetime.

How can we tell of such a thing?
The world is being eaten
by a great monster
too big to imagine.
There is nothing to do
but cast myself into its nets.

Despite all that is Broken

Despite all that is broken
the blackbird still sings
and so, even for those
who plunder the earth
I give thanks
for showing me
how much I love
how much I rage
and how fiercely I will stand
between the blackbird
and the blade.

The Good Ancestor

Every day I walk a hundred years
to the hill where my great great granddaughter sits.
I carry words of blessing
and reach to touch her back

But feeling me near she turns
sad eyed and heavy with grief
"What was it like?" she asks
"when the great whales swam
when the birds sang you awake
when the rains came soft
and the soil smelled sweet underfoot?"
And the blessings
catch in my throat

On darker days she turns,
her famished face charred and eyes,
sunk in their bony orbits,
burn with curses.
And the blessings
froth at my mouth
with the poisonous
spume of betrayal

On the darkest of all days
I walk the hundred years
and find no one there

Let today be the bright day.
Let today be the bright day

I lay my hand upon her back
and, feeling me there, she turns
and blesses me, saying
"Your love was fierce enough,
sweet ancestor, your love
was fierce enough".

The Sun Still Rises

They will not thank you
for your despair
For the tears you spilled
alone that day
with the dying bee
For the days you were
so weighed down by grief
you could not move
For the lovesongs you wrote
to a vanishing world
For your broken heart

Hope sleeps or is dead, we are unsure,
or sealed still in Pandora's jar
yet the sun still rises, as must you
they will thank you only for what you do.

Badger

Crow ups from the splattered
brains of badger
steam pressed into tarmac
not long ago
shouldering myopic
through the intimate darkness
toward this violent end
in a howl of light

No more the snouting clan trails
through the shining scent pierced night
No more the claw ripped bark,
glanded signpost
to the grubbing fields
No more the sharp stench of vole
amongst the snuffling tussocks,
the soft crunch of snail in the mouth
and moon bathing worms
in the feasting meadows

Our onward headlit rush
toward far destinations
crosses a darker and slower geography
invisible until this sudden
collision of worlds

My son asks only
why the badger crossed the road
like some dark joke
She didn't I reply
we crossed hers.

Desire Lines

The road no longer loves the land
its old lines broken, the new
more brutally convenient.

No memory rises from
the path we walk, no footstep
marks where we have been

no revelation on a journey
too fast for conversation
with the small gods of place.

The road follows the desire lines
of our frantic mind, across a land
insulted by our passing

and signposts signal only
what we lose, as we rush
across the graveyard of history
toward the final forgetting.

Blackbird

In the café
my mind casts its net for a poem.
I capture a blackbird
and gather it into this page.
When it sings
its song of gratitude
for the light, for the worm,
for the trees of the great Up,
I imagine this as the last blackbird
and this its last song
before all things
are folded in darkness
forever. And the blackbird says
'Write this down.
I am always singing the last song.'

Diagnosis

I have seen them turn
toward life, those the doctor
sentences to death
their diagnosis beyond doubt
cancer's image irrefutable

I have seen them turn
to those they love
finally opened to cherishing
and being cherished
stubborn refusals dissolving at last
into belonging

I have seen them turn
away from all that harms
the ground on which they stand
the body in which they live
extend the span
of the one life
they have finally
come to love
I have seen them open
to joy

I have seen them stop
their hungry gnawing at the world
to breathe the sea air
to touch the tree
to bow before the flower
turning toward something

more eloquent
and simple

I have seen them smile
at the incandescent
and irresistible
beauty of the world
speaking of love
and its necessity
some arriving as they leave
some turning the disease around
and entering a second
more passionate
and grateful life
I have seen those too
who refuse the invitation

The news that changes everything
is no longer whispered
but shouted across the earth.
Now that we know
beyond doubt
the dying we face
what will we do?

I ask again
What will we do?

Red List

I remember the white slabs
in ordered rows, stone pages
from the book of carnage
remember his name
in the register of the dead
and how we knelt
at our ancestor's grave
wordless, each delving
into bone memory
grateful and appalled
to sit at last
in the aftermath
of the vast tsunami
that was 1918.

He had at least
the dignity of a name.
So many graves
for the unknown soldier
and more still buried
in the relentless mud
never found or given
this small acknowledgment
of a life cut short.

But no grave today
for the sixty percent
of mammals, birds, fish, reptiles
gone in my lifetime
nowhere to kneel

no monument,
just increments of absence
in an emptying playground
and too often now
the absolute silences
of extinction.

The Red List
tries to keep pace
with the fallen
but the bodies pile higher.
Whoever reads this
when we are gone
will not name it
the sixth mass extinction
as we do, as if
we bore no part
but instead
the unholiest of all wars
declared against
every creature on earth.

LIGHT ON
THE HORIZON

Earth Drum

Along these cliffs
they too looked out
on the ceaseless motion of the sea,
ancestors we never knew,
who hauled from the ground
the heavy rocks now piled
as walls or planted upright
to make the toothed boundary
lunging precariously down the steep headland,
their round huts porous
to the incessant breath of the sea
and prying winds,
speaking to me now through my feet
as I walk in their vanishing footprints.

A hundred times I have walked here
but still a visitor.
It would take a lifetime of bowing
to this land in all its seasons
before the buzzard,
seen today hovering keenly on the wind's edge,
accepts me as cousin.
Yet I know I love this place.
Here I have exchanged vows
with the wild shore
and the crazed headlands
and rolling fields
a pact of love

that brings me back
again and again
as it has today.

I gaze out beyond the arced rib of the horizon.
Across the water at Standing Rock
the nations of the first people
rise again,
the beat of the earth's drum
calling them toward
the canons of the new cavalry.
Sacred ground, sacred ground
In all our bones
sleeps a warrior
who has never
abandoned the earth.

I don't know if love is enough.
The rip tide of despair
can pull us far from the shore
pulls me now
toward its loveless drowning.
Going down to the pebbled beach
I close my eyes
my back to the rocks
my face bathed
in the pale warmth of the winter sun.
I feel the dread of the monstrous force
rising in the west.

I do not know
whether loving this world
is enough to save it.
But I do know
that whatever we do not love enough
we will lose.

Light on the Horizon

We woke to fierce winds
hurling spray toward the window
a sky heaving with cloud
clambering out of the south
dragging its tails in the sea
and trawling far inland

At the land's edge
I watch the waves
unravelling against the rocks,
the cold moil and sweat
of the waters churning
in crevices, the spume
lifted high on the wind

A wild day
and I have come down
to stand in its open jaw

Out beyond the turmoil
I watch for whatever weather is rising
beyond where sea and sky
struggle to separate.
There is no telling

Nor could it have been told
that the clouds would crack just enough
as they did, splaying columns of sunlight
in an immense fan far out at sea
a thin bar of light igniting along the horizon

and the distant waters burning
as if I stood in another time
witness to the miraculous birth of fire
at the edge of the visible world

I want to tell of this
in words ripped from my mouth
by the crazed wind
carrying the news to other lives
equally in need of saving.

Renewal

An hour before dawn and I have walked
to the headland wrapped against cold
to watch and wait for the old reassurance.

Across a fathomless sky pierced by stars
squalls of blueblack clouds
spread like squid ink.
Below me the last fishing boats wink
along the reef, soon to haul
their cold harvest to shore.

Slowly the signs come of a waking world:
a cormorant's dark silhouette flying low,
the first creak and craw of seagull
and the looming rocks taking form
far out in the bay.

The time is near.
I stand as if to applaud, or sing
but do neither. Instead
a sudden inward breath
like the newborn's first
raw and astonished gasp
as the earth tips eastward
the underedge of clouds catches fire
and the sun rises dripping from the underworld.

Sure now of renewal
I can turn homeward.

Two Cormorants

Troubled times
and I have come again
to the edge of this land
to stand at the shore
where the waters seethe
over jagged rocks.
I have come to see
what is written
on the sea
spread now
like a vast sheet
of flecked paper
between shore
and horizon.
This is where
I empty myself
of questions
This is where
I ask nothing
and everything
This is where I wait

From the east
two cormorants
fly low
across the water
with linear intent
two words
inscribed across
an empty page

an inscrutable
and eloquent
oracle

It is answer enough
It is answer enough

Breath

The breath that gives flight to the bird
gives life to me
dust that once was stars
shines in my bones
and the word that once was god
speaks with my mouth, saying
whatever made the daffodil
made me too.

Snowdrops

You might want to prise the heart open.
There are tools for that, tools
to bend bars, break down doors
and people willing to wield the weapons
in the name of love.
Forgive them their apparent violence.
They mean well, I think.

Or go instead
to the young snowdrops clustered
along the riverbank
and ask them if they know a gentler way.
They have something to say
about wonder which is worthy
of your attention.

Go now, while the window is ajar.
Grace is near.

Time

Five o'clock.
And yet there is another time
than the one that crowds me here
myopic with its small urgencies
its seductions and
broken rhythms

And so I perform the necessary rituals
walking out into the day
near, far, whatever is needed
to remember again
the cycles to which I belong

Like today, at Prawle again
across the headland soil, cold
with winters slow gestation
I walk past tight blackthorn
on the cusp of its Imbolc flowering
past pale primrose already signalling
the return of the light.
The world
on the sling of its orbit
has already begun
its long slow leaning
back toward the sun

On the shore I rake among pebbles
each one a small moon cast by the sea
There is another rhythm working here
dictated by the cold lunar pull

an older rhythm, before seasons
before the palpable time of growth
and decay, before soil

I light a driftwood fire
huddled close as the world empties
of the frail warmth of this January day
and look up into the deepening dark
as the stars increase
and time loses its anchorage.
I look out, beyond time now
backward toward our beginning

Small sparks drift,
flicker and are gone.
Sometimes it takes
a dark night
like this
to know our place
in the great unfolding
and the small
bright mark
we make
in time.

Scorhill

Evening at the stone circle,
a constellation of granite
speaking a language forgotten,
syllables of a stone alphabet
from an age more literate.
I take my place.

Below me the darkening cows
have slowed and gathered
to stand the night
amongst the sweet marsh grasses.
A distant cacophony of rooks
tumbles into the trees
over Fernworthy
and a solitary bat
flits and dips
in and out of vision
as the last colours
dance themselves out.
Along the horizon
the tors turn black as peat.

I settle wrapped in a blanket
back to the stone,
folded into the gathering darkness,
the ebb light
brimming with revelation,
the stones leaning
in silent conversation
with the stars.

I am alone
with the ghosts of ancestors,
whatever they knew
written into the land,
loveletters to the earth
from long ago.
We sit together watching
the slow wheel of the sky
unafraid of the dark
or one another
knowing how
in the unveiling night
the eye begins to see.

A Road Home

Even for those who rip out its heart
the world is always near.
A man setting down his chainsaw
sees a wild flower
or stepping away from the bulldozer
looks up at a flight of birds
and something brushes his heart.

For all our turning away
we are never truly lost.
It will be like this until the end
the world always near
and hidden in each moment
an opening to wonder,
a road home.

THE STORY GOES

Back Rooms

Really, they are not very interesting.
The room we are in now is best.
In the others I keep parts of me
you have never met,
parts even I have never visited.

You say you want to hold my hand
in the dark and scary rooms
but I am afraid you will drown
in the one full of tears
and recoil from the room
stuffed with dead angels.
And what of the loveless rooms
or the ones where you find me
fucking someone else?

There are more comfortable rooms
you might enjoy:
some where the sea lives
and trees and grasshoppers,
rooms full of birdsong
and the scent of bluebells
one room humming with bumble bees
another home to a goddess
who hugs all who enter.

There are rooms stacked high with half written poems
rooms where abandoned thoughts still unravel
rooms opening onto roads not taken
and a locked room full of daleks.

Some rooms have been squatted
by versions of me I no longer recognise.
Some are empty.

Rooms full of ancestors
in one room my own death
in another a gateway to the next life

These days I camp in the front room
and visit them rarely.
Really, they are not very interesting.

Let's open the door
and step into the garden.

Burial

This morning I felt his presence again,
the one I buried.
Too late to turn away now.
Though my legs would run
though my mind would close
though my heart would shut its doors
they could not.
I was already kneeling at his grave.

I saw him push
against the heavy stone slab.
He could feel the pull of the sun
hear birds singing
smell the teeming earth
the life not to be denied.

I laid my hand on the gravestone
possessed by a terrifying impulse.
Imagine my surprise then:
not the rotten stink of the corpse
nor the unbearable howl of rage and grief
not the leaping revenge of the one I had abandoned.

No, she, naked and beautiful
smiling at me, invites me in.
I left my clothes by the headstone
and climbed down.

Inseparable now we walk through the day hand in hand.
I have no words for this happiness

or, if I could find them
they would be made of sunlight on leaves
the angle of a bird's wing
the smell of rain.

Apple

A fallen apple fills
my seven year old hand
one half edible still
the other bruised already
to the core.

They cannot see me.
The old Bramley is out back
on the windowless side of the house.

When it hits the wall
with a wet splat and spit
the air bursts from my lungs
and I throw again and again
until I stand alone, spent
and empty handed
startled by the taste
of this new knowledge.

As if in answer
the sun fled behind a cloud
and a shadow swept
through the garden
quiet and cold as an eclipse.

It comes again on abandoned days
when I cannot stay my hand.
And shame smells of rotting fruit
from the places I long ago
tried to hide from god.

Remembrist

They say on the seventh day
God sat back to admire his masterpiece.
Well, I don't know about the god thing
but I do know that in plain sight
the people came and one by one
rubbed out its exquisite detail
-and, my god, it was exquisite-
one by one the butterflies and gleaming beetles,
the tiniest flowers. They stripped
the land of trees. One day
they even erased the great whales from the sea.
On the last day they took out colour.
Are we the only ones who noticed?

These days, the few of us who remain,
we call ourselves the Remembrists.
They call us Fantasists with our childlike tales
of mythical creatures.
But remembering becomes hard, becomes hard.
We cling to the miraculous possibility
that we can dream it all awake again.
It is all we have.
How else can we live?

Meter Man

He came to read the meter today
stooping into the cupboard
before I registered much
except his bald head and good humour
in the dark chaos beneath the stairs.
It was only when he rose
and left me with "God bless"
(and left with no assumption
of his own importance)
that I was suddenly touched.
God bless he said
a door so quickly opened and closed
a spill of light into the hallway
and me still standing
blessed before I even knew how much
I stood in need of blessing.

Carrying Embers

The story goes that the hearth fire
of this highest pub on the moors
has been kept alight
three hundred years.
We want to believe it
and one story
kindles another.

Once, I tell them, a man
brought to our campfire
a ten thousand year stick
plucked by an African tribe
from the embers
of each dying fire
and used to start the next.

And once upon a time, says another
across the moors here
the old tribes carried embers
from camp to camp smouldering
in hardened fungus,
each fire seeded by its mother.

And once a lone priest wandered
tor to tor carrying in his heart
the fire of Christ kept alive
since Galilee.

We settle into silence
the firelight in our eyes.

We saw it then
though none spoke it:
something burns in each of us
not our own,
old as time.

The Small Flower

The small flower opened its petals
and by its exquisite shining
called me to sit beside it.
And the small flower spoke, saying
"I am the last of my kind.
Please stay with me in my dying."
So I sat and stayed
and the days passed
and I watched the small flower
swell in the final exuberance
of its life.

And the small flower said
"I will not come again.
I will live in your heart
for as long as you remember me
but when you too are gone
I will join the great forgetting."
And the small flower told me
of its ancestors before human time
of the many days dancing in the sunlight
bowing to the rain
sleeping beneath ice
and the long miracle
closing now forever
and I wept
and the first petal fell.

And the small flower in its small voice said
"The time of the great burning

and the crazed winds
and drownings has begun.
The souls of those too tender
to withstand have already
begun their migration into the void.
I go with them now."
And I wept and ached
and heard the crack
of the world breaking.

The Children's Christmas List

For every child, the right to be a child
and a long line of heroes who will stand as shield
against any who would take this from them
For every child without food, an apology and a place at the table
For every child orphaned by war, an explanation written in blood
For every refugee, an unconditional welcome
For the child abused, promises so holy they can never again be broken
For the child trapped in poverty, a fair share
For the child stolen, a homecoming.

On Christmas day let the thieves of childhood
give back all they have taken.

The Still Man

A man so still
the birds fly in and
out of his heart
swallows quick with summer
ragged crows, wrens.

Some bring twigs
choosing his head as home
build nests, rear young
fledglings tumbling out
their flight guided by instincts
written in their bones

Like the new and tentative poems
I now throw from the open window
into the sunlit garden.

TUMBLING TOWARD ANOTHER

A Beginning

A beginning there was for sure.
Your message, a beginning
of rising, a kindling

And earlier beginnings, I remember now
stood still watching you across the grass
something uncoiling inside

Or the hug I asked of you
unable to stop myself, feeling already
the tumbling toward you

Or the way I came to see
your new path, only to be closer to you
beginnings inside beginnings

And the true beginning elsewhere
before we met
before you were born

Perhaps beyond the wombs
of both our beginnings.

In Her Lies the End of all Choosing

Sitting next to you
my body has begun singing.
I have nothing to say.
The decision is already made
in the shimmering cells and softening tissues,
in the deep agreement of my body
with this moment of sitting here with you.

My mind has no argument with this
nor the world. It has withdrawn
into the circulating fluids of the heart
to talk with god.
I notice everything:
the leaning daffodil in the blue vase
stone fireplace, red carpet
and the exact distance between our hands.

The new and fresh page of our lives together lies open.
It is already written that our hands will touch
that though we are almost strangers
we will soon understand
how we have carried each other's portrait
in our hearts all these years
how the whole journey of our lives
has leant towards this moment.

In the long labour of our dreams
we have been building the house together
whose threshold we are about to cross.
Now, following no map

except the heart's tender yearning,
we have arrived in this room
where the dreaming is finally over.

I am awake and you are here at last.
I have reached the shore of my own longing
and the end of all choosing.
In the bright and quiet room
there is nothing more certain
than the rightness
of our two hands
about to touch.

Neighbour

Not yet Spring
but sun in January
the year already turned
and the bulbs pregnant
with this year's flower
swelling and softening
in the dark earth.
I stand outside the house
watching winter's thin light
through the bare oak
the smoke going up
from a friend's hearth
and her crossing the green
turning her head toward me

I watch the sway of her
breasts against the loose jumper
suggesting their soft and perfect forms
and imagine their weight
nesting in my hands.
Her mouth speaks words
but shapes itself like kisses
against my flesh
and her eyes a dark invitation
to a warm and blissful drowning

At night through dream forests
her nakedness stalks me
half revealed, parting the moist leaves
her laughter teasing like sunlight

and all the wild creatures
shrieking their delight
until we tumble
into the place
where I uncoil
and the grip
of the world
releases me

Some lines the imagination crosses
though the body does not.
Our elegant dance
of restrained desire
will have its season,
its ripening and eventual fall

Meanwhile the sap roars
through the stiffening stem
of the wild daffodil
and the bee enters the pollen chamber.

My Body Dreams of Her

I lift my gaze
from the empty page
and open to the new poem
being born on the sun streaked surface
of the morning sea.
I wait for words
drenched in sunlight
and sea spray
for the day's revelation
arriving on the breeze

But it is she who arrives
the one I turned away from
her skin brushing against my face
her scent at my nostrils
now entering my blood again like smoke
more present to me suddenly
than the glistening sea below.

I close my eyes
and surrender
to the body's telling
of unfinished desires
to the ebb and flow of memories
across my skin
let sun and sea carry me
where they will
until I am released again
into the day
a sky daubed with clouds

the wheeling gulls, a kestrel hovering,
light pounding the sea's surface
the lip of the waves at my feet.

I stoop to gather a pebble
roll it between my fingers
loving the roundness of it
its exquisite colour
the way it fits in my hand
as if it might belong
then cast it in a gentle underarm arc
into the waves.

Perhaps the sea will give it back one day
perhaps another hand will
close around its smooth surface
put it in a pocket
take it home.

Night Swan

We are newly lovers
and the long night is full
of the smell of skin and roses.
We have travelled far for this
across the years
of loving, of not loving
to this bright bed
these fat candles
and the cold moonlight
lapping at the window

The night around us is so wide
I can hear far beyond the lake
the beat of the white swan's wings
in the luminous darkness
its neck outstretched like a bar of light
its red pulsing heart wrapped in whiteness
as it journeys home
across the harsh tundra and bitter seas

Meanwhile we ride the long wet night
of our desire
learning each other's bodies
and our own anew
travelling the silken channels of our flesh
towards each other

until in the wild darkness
my wave breaks upon
the new shore of your body

and I am tumbling
like the swan
into the waiting waters

delivered unexpectedly
into innocence
into a bright and lucid
silence

For a moment bewildered
I search your face for answers

I don't know where they come from
these salt tears
it is as if you had spoken
the echo of my own longing

as if the swan had been called
all those thousands of miles
by its own reflection
in the dark water

as if I had been
migrating towards you
all my life.

Coming Home

She is asleep upstairs,
has left on the hall light,
a love token, the imprint
of her love still on the lightswitch
the scent of it in the air of the stairwell.
The house breathes with her
as if under a spell.
I climb the stairs
to stroke her bare shoulder
rousing her slightly
then soothing her back to sleep.
She has laid new sheets on the bed.
Whatever hardness
gripped my heart today
is melting.

Everything Comes and Goes

Everything comes and goes
Nothing comes and stays
Even this love
Even the longest burning

This morning a bullfinch blazing
high in the cherry tree
and you and I huddled
in our years of loving
watching from the bedroom

They are visitors, the quick birds
these joys and griefs too.
And even you, even the spark
that once ignited life,
will fly onward

We live on the cooled crust
of boiling lava beneath a thinning sky.
Our days will end in ice or fire.
Even desire, even this moment
of loving you
has wings

Everything comes and goes
Nothing comes and stays
Even this love
Even the longest burning.

A Place at the Table

I set a place for her
nevertheless, as we did
for the stranger
or unexpected friend

and keep open the window
to catch news of her arrival
setting down my fork each time
the breeze stirs the blue curtain.

Dust has settled thinly
on the windowsill, on the bowl
of pebbles gathered and pocketed
over the years

and the tight fircone
we brought down from the mountain
has opened and the spiders
moved in.

Only the photos on the piano
shine as bright as the day you left,
evidence when judgment comes
of a tended love undimmed by time.

Stone Flower

I ask the stone flower in my heart
what it needs. Give me juice it says.
Touch me with your lips.
Remember me.

INTO THE SPECKLED SILENCE

Thin Air

The air is thin now
between life and death
a few molecules of breath
until the last.

Winds billow over the grass
of old summers
and the faces come and go
the memories of all her days
rising and falling
falling from her now
as she nears the crossing.

The last strands
surrender their anchor
as another more distant gravity
pulls at her soul.

Between each breath
a domed stillness presses
long and slow,
those who wait dropped
deep in their listening
for the last wingbeat
as the guest readies for flight.

Here she goes now
into fields of gold
our Jo, released at last,
her song rippling out
into the infinite light.

After Her Death

How quickly the dead are swallowed
in the forward rush of time
so recently gone and yet
hours without thinking of her.

Maybe this is how it is after death
all of us hurtling onwards
the pace accelerating
the new rushing in
sweeping away the dust
of the dead hours and minutes
as we scramble hopelessly for pause.

Last night I dreamed of her
holding her hand as she gasped
the last startled breath
but in our dreamworld
where death can be cheated
I willed her corpse to dance
again, her mouth to laugh.

I don't want to sit with her body.
What use does the dragonfly have
for its discarded shell?
Although, yes, I have held one
in my hand and marvelled
how the new body has flown.

Or was it otherwise, her death
a pressing against a wall

that cannot be passed through?
A dead end with no surrender,
no peace made with the fury,
an extinction beyond which nothing survives;
our hope for something more
as fragile as the dragonfly's husk.

For Colin

You old talk too much jay bird you
your whitening beard bright as its vanishing rump
so much to say even now
unearthing memories like the acorns you planted
in the diligently tended forest of your life

You broke cover in those last days
let us see the treasured turquoise
feather in your wing bend
a flash of light between the worlds
shy as the first smile we coaxed from you

You elusive old crow cousin you
revealing your true colours at last.

God's Shadow

We sit in circle
with the man
who has been sentenced to die
the swollen seed of his dying
buried deep in his brain
each of us helpless
and wanting to help
each of us alone and
wanting to know reasons
but the cancer's secret
is his alone
the final conversation private
and wordless

We are men, together
called to support a brother
offering the muscle of our attention
and all that is lovely in men
our silence
the sword of enquiry
a flock of words from the open heart
hands that touch to the bone
a dark and fierce humour
our readiness to lean far out into the night

I want to scream at him to fight
I want to fight for him
want to make it all not so
anything but this
my friend, my brother

leaving
the dead man walking

Cancer
this is the dark work
the shadow eating at life
inside the tumour
the fiery Christ
performs his ministry
within the Christ
the old god gleaming
within the old god
the choir of mad souls
and in their voices
the beautiful yellow of the first daffodil
the world is fierce and beautiful

I think of these
malignant cells, disaffected
such inner terrorists
the bombs of modern medicine
cannot heal.
In the cancerous cell is god's shadow
pregnant with everything
that cannot be made godly

We offer him
the cauldron of the heart
where all shadow is
illuminated

where everything we cannot speak
is cremated

Yet even this surrender to the heart
may not be enough
our dying is with us already
the mystery is defiant
and radiant
no joy without suffering
no suffering without joy
no life without death
no death without life
no ending without beginning

I saw the look in his eye
and had no answer
I pray for readiness
I pray for consumption by fire
I pray for anything but this bewilderment
in the face of death

And so the dead man went home.
Our conversation turned then
to other things
as much to leave behind
what we could not bear
as to affirm our own aliveness
and the necessity
of life moving on

And I move on now
turning from the page
towards the day.
With this small poem
finally completed
I remember you, James
and lay you to rest
again.

Migration

Sometimes I think it must be like this,
the migration of souls

The way geese come over the visible horizon
honking with delight and recognition
and how they leave, long necks outstretched
toward a future we cannot see

Sometimes I think it must be like this
a brief exuberance between
arrival and departure
wings that know the way
we are blind to.

Winter Rose

Standing this morning on the doorstep
a few petals lie scattered
fallen from the pale winter rose
hanging in the fragile sunlight.
And I think how slender
our hold on life
how light our crossing into death
how beautiful our brief
and fragrant existence

Later, digging out elder
I think how tenacious
our holding to this world
how fierce the will to live
how every moment in this garden
is a wild jamboree of incarnation
mad as India

How weightless our dying
petals falling from the stem
How passionate our rooting
deep into this earth.

Pearlmaker

Many hours watching the sea
in all its seasons
its meditations and ecstatic dances
combing the shore for each tide's gifts
pebbles rolled and polished
fragments of shell
and in my hand today
the nacreous gleam of oyster

Anchored to the seabed
a precious few make pearls
in small dark chambers
sucking sea through cold lips
building layer on layer
while moons come and go

Like the great masters
who cultivated pearls
in the secret chambers
of their own bodies
a condensation of light
anchored by mind
polished by the tidal abrasion of breath
raked from their ashes
on the final shore of their lives.

Companion

After the long night
of my mother's labour
a blackbird sang
from the windowsill
at the dawn of my birth.

Along the way now
they are companions,
bright eyed fossickers
in leaf litter,
singers after rain.

A pair nest each year
in the bay tree close by the house
and migrants come in winter
to peck at the fallen apples
I leave for them.

All my life
we have paid attention
to one another, familiars
on our journeys
between worlds.

One day perhaps,
just as he sang me in,
the blackbird will sing me back
into the speckled silence
of another night.

The Last Move

You know you've lost
the last move was never yours
your strategy overwhelmed
by the gods who never
play by the rules
you thought would keep you safe